A Gander Called Vlad and the Train in the Sky

Story and illustrations

by Lily Beetle

Copyright © 2024 Diana Eddy

All rights reserved.

For Jodie

CONTENTS

1	Something Under the Bed	Pg 1
2	A Gander Called Vlad	Pg 6
3	Grandad Makes a Deal	Pg 24
4	A Glint of Gold	Pg 40
5	Skippy's Café	Pg 54
6	Red Riding Hood and the Rocking Horse	Pg 65
7	Luke	Pg 80
8	Some Very Angry Geese	Pg 84
9	A Mystery Solved	Pg 89
10	The Man from the BBC	Pg 100
11	A Happy Surprise	Pg 110

Chapter 1
Something Under the Bed

I feel the mattress heave underneath me. There is definitely, something, under the bed. Outside a lone firework goes BANG. The mattress heaves again and I hear a whimpering noise coming from below. I grip the edge of my blanket and feel the hair prickling on the back of my neck.

The only light in the bedroom is coming from the landing, through my open bedroom door. But surely the door had been all but closed, except for a crack, when Aunty Pru had tucked me in and said goodnight.

A hot wave of fear is trickling down my back. My heart feels like it is trying to escape from my chest. I feel the mattress heave again; I think I might faint! I try and remember my favourite things, like Maria, in the *Sound of Music* [1] but my mind has gone blank.

"Monty, Monty, where are you?" I hear Aunty Pru

calling from downstairs.

"Stupid boys, letting off fireworks on the Green and it's not even Guy Fawkes night yet," she continues. "Poor Monty will be scared stiff." I can hear Uncle Derek replying to her, in a muffled voice, from the sitting room.

"Monty, Monty, here boy, come to mummy," Pru calls softly up the stairs.

More whimpering sounds come from under the bed. I summon all my courage and peer over the edge of the mattress and underneath the bed. A sad pair of yellow eyes look back at me and a long, wet tongue tries to lick my face.

"Oh Monty!" I cry, so relieved. "What are you doing hiding under my bed?"

In answer, Aunty Pru's chocolate brown Labrador dog, crawls out of his hiding place and immediately attempts to get onto the bed with me.

"Gerroff!" I say, laughing, as he licks my face. Monty takes the laughing as an invitation and heaves his large body onto the bed, accidently pinning me helplessly against the wall. I have a face full of fur and have to push against him hard to work myself free. But Monty now looks very content as he stretches his long legs out in front of him, and places his head on his paws.

He looks expectantly at me with his big yellow eyes. He shifts his eyebrows up and down and beats his tail on my pillow in a half wag.

BANG! Whizz! another firework lights up the sky behind the closed curtains. Monty's face freezes with fear, his ears flatten and he squeezes his body against mine. Aunty Pru appears at the door.

"Monty?" she calls softly, "Are you in there?"

"Yes, Aunty Pru, he's in here!" I call with difficulty from my flattened position, "Monty was under the bed, he must have been scared of the fireworks!"

Aunty Pru switches on the top light; I blink in the sudden glare.

"Ridiculous animal!" she scolds, grabbing Monty by the collar and heaving him off the bed. "His father was a champion gun dog, very valuable animal, quarter finalist at Crufts. This one is terrified if you talk too loudly!"

Monty looks ashamed. Aunty Pru fishes in the pocket of

her cardigan and pulls out a dog biscuit; Monty delicately nibbles it from her hand.

"I mean," continues Aunty Pru, fussing his ears, "whoever heard of a gundog who is afraid of loud noises!"

Aunty Pru is my mum's aunt. I am being a 'brave girl' and staying with her and Uncle Derek (and Monty) for the week. This is so Mum and Dad can go and stay in a hotel in Yorkshire and visit a petrified waterfall. But I don't understand why a waterfall should be scared and I double don't understand why I couldn't go and stay in the hotel too.

I am trying to be a 'brave girl,' but it is very tiring when you are six years old and home sick.

"Well night, night, then Molly," says Aunty Pru, dragging a reluctant Monty through the door. "Don't let the bed bugs bite," she says cheerily switching the top light off and firmly closing the door. She has forgotten to leave it open just a crack.

When I hear her footsteps reach the downstairs, I tip toe out of bed and open the door just enough to let the light in. I hurry back to bed. Then I remember the bed bugs that Aunty Pru was saying about, so I get my tiny torch from under the pillow and have a good look under the blankets. But it is OK, there is nothing there.

I find Doggy, my pink cuddly dog and snuggle back down the bed.

"Night Doggy," I say out loud, so it feels real. Then reluctantly I turn off the torch.

Bed time is not the same without Dad's special tucking in so that the Sea Monsters from *Dr Who* [2] can't get me. At home the Sea Monsters are just for fun and I know they are not real. But here, in Aunty Pru's old farmhouse, with its strange shadows and strange noises, everything scary feels real.

Outside a fox barks; it sounds like a woman screaming. I hold doggy close and scrunch my eyes tight shut. I will never get to sleep.

But the bed is warm and soft and it is hard work staying alert, listening for every tiny noise that may or may not be normal and I am so very tired. In no time at all my head fills with pleasant pictures of unicorns and baby foals, all with big yellow eyes and sparklers for tails. The stresses of the day seem far away as I slip into a deep and dream filled sleep.

Chapter 2
A Gander Called Vlad

"Molly! Time to get up!" Aunty Pru calls up the stairs.
I open my eyes and am surprised to see daylight through a crack in the curtains. I wonder at my being such a scaredy-cat last night and make a promise to myself not to be afraid anymore.

I slip my pony calendar from under my pillow.

"The 28th October 1976," I read out slowly. There is a sad face around the date. It is the first day of the half term. I should be with Mum and Dad doing fun things like going to the park and playing on the swings and the banana slide. Or riding on Dad's bike or doing baking with Mum.

I slip out of bed and pad barefoot across the polished wooden floor boards towards the window. The floor is cold under my feet.

I pull the heavy curtains aside and stand on tip toe to see out of the window.

Below is the abandoned farmyard. No cows, or pigs, or horses or tractors, just empty barns and styes and stables. It makes me feel sad.

Aunty Pru and Uncle Derek retired from farming last year. When they retired, they sold all the animals and machinery. A long time ago Aunty Pru even had a horse called Toby; she used to lift me up and let me stroke him.

I loved Toby. He had a velvety nose with bristles, that used to sniff my hand and make me giggle. But now it is like a ghost farm. All that is left are a few chickens for their eggs, and a heard of angry geese, that seem to have no purpose at all.

I wonder if it makes Aunty Pru and Uncle Derek feel sad as well. Of course, they are not my real aunty and uncle, they are Mum's aunty and uncle, so they are my great aunty and uncle. But Mum said it was OK if I called them aunty and uncle, as putting 'great' in front of everything makes too much of a mouthful.

Mum used to come and stay on the farm when she was a little girl. She used to ride Toby and make dens in the spinney, by the stream, with her cousin Sally (Aunty Pru and Uncle Derek's daughter).

I think Mum got the best deal; I wish I had someone to play with. I feel suddenly lonely in this big grownup bedroom, with its grownup furniture and grownup curtains.

I miss my little room at home with my moon and stars nightlight and my sunflower curtains.

"Woof, woof, woof!" Monty bursts from the back door like a cannon ball and runs excitedly across the gravel drive and into the paddock.

His ears are flapping as he runs madly towards the spinney and the stream. A blanket of mist still covers the end of the paddock, but above the trees the sun is bright in a hard blue sky. The beech trees in the spinney reach their branches up though the mist, with leaves clinging to the twigs like bright orange flames.

Monty has nearly reached the spinney. He has left a happy trail of footprints in the dew drenched grass. But he comes skidding to an abrupt halt, as a big white gander steps out of the trees and blocks his path. It lowers its head, snaking its neck in a menacing way.

Monty wags his tail uncertainly, but the gander raises his wings and charges at Monty. He nips at Monty's legs with his hard orange beak. Monty yelps and scrabbles backwards, but the rest of the geese swarm out of the shrubbery behind him all flapping their wings and honking mercilessly.

Poor Monty looks like he is trapped! But he dives sideways and runs yelping, with his tail between his legs, back to the house.

The big white gander turns to the other geese, with his

head held high, honking proudly. They gather around him with much excited flapping, congratulating him on his victory.

"What a bully!" I say, "Poor Monty!

"Yes, he is rather," says Aunty Pru from behind me.

I jump like a scared cat.

"Oh, my dear!" she says. "I didn't mean to make you jump."

"That's OK, Aunty Pru," I gasp laughing. But I still feel a bit jangly, like an empty wardrobe full of metal coat hangers.

"He'll have to go of course," says Aunty Pru, joining me by the window.

"Who Monty?" I say, astonished.

"No silly," says Aunty Pru, "Vlad the Impaler down there. That horrible big gander. Your Uncle Derek brought him from a farm sale at Burnt End and he has been a menace since the day he arrived. We had the geese first and they used to be quite docile. But then Vlad arrived and got them all riled up and now they are as militant as he is."

"Oh," I say, "that doesn't sound very good."

"No good indeed," sighs Pru. "The post man refuses to come down the drive since Vlad and his wives got him in a pincer movement by the back door. Vlad got his beak fastened on the poor man's calf and wouldn't let go.

Luckily your Uncle Derek got there in the nick of time and pulled Vlad off him before he actually drew blood. The trick is to grab them round the neck, just under the head, then they can't peck you."

"I'll try and remember that," I say nervously.

"In any case," says Aunty Pru, smiling down at me, "breakfast is ready, so get dressed and come down to the kitchen." She leaves the room humming tunelessly to herself.

I look at my clothes lying neatly on the back of the chair; my blue jeans, white T-shirt and pink cardigan with the flower shaped buttons. The clothes look small and empty on the smooth wooden chair, like the shell of a girl. Or a girl snake who has shed her skin.

Slowly I dress; the cardigan buttons are fiddly and my socks have bobbly bits in the toe, so I have to take them off and try again. I find my black school Plimsolls, with the stretchy elastic bits at the side and pull them on my feet.

Mum says I must wear indoor shoes at Aunty Pru's house and not to go around in my 'stockinged feet'. She says that as all the floors are made of wood or stone they can get very cold, even in October and I don't want to be getting 'chilled brains'. Well I don't wear stockings, I wear socks and my brain isn't in my feet it is in my head. When I tried to tell Mum she just said that I would understand when I was older and to hurry up and get ready to go.

I have noticed that grownups are always in a hurry to go somewhere and they always make you hurry as well. 'Hurry up and get ready for school,' or 'Hurry up and have your bath,' or 'Hurry up and get ready for bed.' It's like there are not enough hours in the day for them to do everything they are supposed to do in a day, so that they have to hurry all the time to keep up.

I brush my hair like Mum showed me, but it goes static and sticks up in the air and turns into knots. So I find a bobble band in my wash bag and tie it back in a pony tail, the best I can. I look in the dressing table mirror and a sad face, with a wonky pony tail looks back.

I tuck Doggy safely under the covers of the bed and set off out of my room and down the corridor, in search of the bathroom.

The house is very old and smells of wax polish and a cold hard smell like stone. It is filled with a sort of empty stillness, like someone has just stopped talking or someone has just left the room.

I find the bathroom and manage to use the toilet. The flush is on a long chain, I pull it hard and the water gurgles down loudly.

When I come out of the bathroom, I can't remember which way to turn. The house is so big that the landing is long and goes round corners with several doors and other passage ways coming off.

I can feel myself beginning to panic. I stop mid-step, I can hear purring like a cat.

I feel like a tiny mouse in a giant's castle. I cross the landing and notice that one of the bedroom doors is slightly open. I start in fright as I see a pair of black beady eyes looking back at me out of the room. I stand rigid and hold my breath; it takes a few seconds to realize that the eyes are not alive, but belong to a furry face; a cuddly dog or bear or something.

I breath out in relief and tiptoe towards the partly open door and push it open wider. The black beady eyes belong to a giant teddy bear sitting on a little chair. Feeling a little braver I push the door wide enough for me to slip into the room.

"Oh my!" I say, as I take it all in. It is a child's room, full of toys. The wall paper is powder blue and patterned with pictures of old-fashioned aeroplanes and hot air balloons.

A tabby cat is sitting on the bed licking its fur. It looks at me as I enter the room, it has one blue eye and one yellow eye and stares steadily at me.

"Beg your pardon," I say, "I didn't mean to disturb you Mr. Cat."

The cat looks up and turns his head to one side, as if he can hear someone calling, then jumps silently from the bed and pads out of the door.

"Oh well," I say sadly. It would have been nice to make friends. But I soon forget my disappointment as I look around the room.

There is a train set on the floor with a green clockwork engine just waiting to be wound up. At the end of the bed there is a big toy box, with toy planes and tin soldiers arranged on top.

There is also a shelf full of picture books. They all look quite old fashioned, but probably still good to look at.

In the corner there is a small desk with pictures and drawings pined to the wall above and more toy planes dangling from the ceiling on cotton threads.

"I wonder who this room belongs too?" I say excitedly. "Maybe there is another cousin, of my age, who I could play with. Maybe it's a surprise?"

"Molly?" I hear Aunty Pru calling up the stairs, "are you managing alright dear?"

I carefully creep outside the room and pull the door gently closed behind me.

"Just coming," I call, "I got a bit lost."

"Can you find your way?" she calls.

I follow where her voice is coming from and find the stairs. I think of the unfriendly, grownup, room that Aunty Pru has given me and wish that I could sleep in the cozy room filled with books and toys.

I walk carefully down the polished wooden stairs and find Aunty Pru waiting at the bottom. We walk along the passageway and into the red brick, floored kitchen.

"Now, I have picked you a bowl of lovely fresh autumn raspberries, straight from the garden," says Aunty Pru.

"It's been so mild recently that they are still cropping. So you really are in luck!"

I slide onto the kitchen chair and look at the bowl of raspberries in front of me, on the table. The bowl of raspberries looks back.

I know I don't like raspberries. I don't like their squishiness or their pips or the look of the tiny hairs which cover them. They look like the tiny hairs that Mrs. Spinks, at the shop, has on her top lip.

Uncle Derek is already sitting at the table, breakfast finished, doing the crossword in his newspaper. He sits there chewing the end of the pen, staring hard at the clues, muttering and sighing under his breath.

"A full-length garment worn by the clergy," he suddenly says. "Seven letters, got an S in it and ends in a K."

"Cossack," says Aunty Pru firmly, from the other side of the kitchen.

"No, no, no," says Derek. "A Cossack is one of those Russian fellas that wear fur hats, and dance squatting down with their arms folded. I've seen them on the TV."

"That's not a Cossack, that's a hassock!" says Aunty Pru indignantly.

"No, you're getting confused," retorts Uncle Derek. "A hassock is what you kneel on in church when you say your prayers."

"That's not a hassock, that's a cassock!" says Aunty Pru, clattering a pan loudly into a cupboard.

"Cassock, that's it! Well done my dear," says Uncle Derek winking at me. "A full-length garment worn by the clergy is a C-A-S-S-O-C-K," he says as he writes the letters into the crossword.

"Well that's what I said in the first place!" says Aunty Pru, swatting crossly, at a lazy fly with her T-towel.

BEEP, BEEP. A car sounds its horn on the drive outside. I can just see the top of a black car, through the kitchen window, as it drives past. We hear Vlad and his wives set up a loud honking and flapping.

A car door slams and someone says "Get out of it!" in a booming voice. We hear the back door open then someone calls, "Anybody at home?"

"In the kitchen, Harold," calls Derek.

A tall figure in Wellington boots, a trilby hat and an army great coat fills the doorway.

"Grandad Green!" I say excitedly.

"Why it's Miss Molly!" he says in a friendly booming sort of way. "And how are you enjoying your stay with your Aunty Pru and Uncle Derek?"

"Very well thank you," I say in a small polite voice, suddenly feeling very home sick.

"Cup of tea Harold?" says Pru. Before waiting for a reply, she bustles to the kitchen dresser for an extra cup and saucer.

"Oh, yes please Pru," says Grandad, settling himself at the table. "Still having trouble with those geese then?" he says.

I sigh heavily, feeling invisible, as the grownups chatter away. The bowl of raspberries is still looking at me. I push them around with my spoon hoping that this will somehow reduce their number.

I feel a cold nose prodding my leg and look down to see two sad yellow eyes looking up at me from under the table. I smile down at Monty and stroke his warm head. He prods my leg again and gives me a hungry look.

I slip one of the raspberries into my hand and hold it under the table; the raspberry disappears into Monty's mouth. I feel a surge of hope. I pick up two more raspberries and slip my hand back under the table. Once more the raspberries disappear from my hand into Monty's mouth.

After three more minutes work, all the raspberries have been transported from my bowl, into Monty's tummy. Both of us are very happy with this exchange.

I clatter my spoon into my now empty bowl. Aunty Pru looks up from the sink.

"That was fast work Molly," she says. "Would you like a boiled egg and toasted soldiers? The water is hot in the pan."

"Oh yes please," I say happily. "Boiled eggs are my favourite."

Aunty Pru clicks at the gas hob to re-boil the water in the egg pan. Meanwhile Uncle Derek and Grandad continue with their conversation.

"There's been trouble at the Hovertrain and at the Dig, each side blaming the other, apparently," says Grandad.

"What sort of trouble?" asks Derek.

"You know the sort of thing," continues Grandad "funny noises in the night, broken fences, bins kicked over, rubbish strewn all over the place. I reckon both sides would be glad of a bit of extra security."

Grandad takes a swig of his tea. "Got any sugar Pru?" he asks.

"Sorry Harold I always forget," she says distractedly, passing him the sugar bowl from the dresser.

Grandad lifts the lid of the sugar bowl and frowns down at the contents.

"Did you know that there is a dead wasp in this sugar bowl Pru?" he says.

"Is it decapitated?" says Pru.

"Yes, it is," says Grandad.

"Oh, yes then," continues Pru. "That's the one I killed the other day."

"Probably time I gave up taking sugar in my tea," says Grandad replacing the lid on the sugar bowl.

"What's a Hovertrain Grandad?" I ask.

"It runs on an 'experimentalist' railway they've built over at Bagford, called a Monorail. The rail runs along the side of the Old Bagford Cut towards Glutton Salt."

"Oh!" I say excitedly. "Can we go for a ride on it?"

Grandad smiles. "It's not ready for people to travel on yet, it's like a full-sized model. All very futuristic, like something that you'd see on your *Star Trek* [3]."

"The Hovertrain runs along the Monorail using magnets apparently," says Uncle Derek, "so that the train doesn't actually touch the rail, just sort of glides above it. That way it can go faster, as there is no friction. They reckon they can get up to 300 miles per hour out of it. Hence the name 'Hovertrain'."

"Hovertrain indeed!" says Aunty Pru, carrying my plate of boiled egg and toasted soldiers over to the table. "More like a white elephant! And the amount of electricity it uses. As if we didn't have enough pressure put on the supply with strikes and oil shortages and wires breaking. There are enough power cuts as it is without that thing sucking up any electric that is left!"

"The price of progress my dear," says Uncle Derek.

"Progress!" says Aunty Pru, suddenly going pink at the ears and stripping off her cardigan. "Mavis Bluebottle reckons it interferes with her radio. Every time she settles down to listen to *The Shipping Forecast* [4], she ends up with 'Dennis Rhesus' blaring out at her."

"Demis Roussos," says Derek.

"That's what I said!" says Pru. "Brenda Spatchcock swears blind that it caused a power surge that made her vacuum cleaner go berserk. She was doing the living room carpet and it lunged right out of her hands; it managed to suck itself half way up the curtains before she managed to pull the plug out!"

"I'm confused," says Grandad. "Was it Demis Roussos, or the Hovertrain that caused the power surge?"

Aunty Pru gives him a hard stare. "All I know is that every time they run the test on that Hovertrain, bad things happen!"

"I've also heard that it makes the milk curdle, dogs howl and birds fly backwards," says Derek.

"Now you're just being silly Derek," scolds Aunty Pru. "It's a ridiculous waste of taxpayers' money and no good will come of it."

"I reckon with all this bad feeling towards them, maybe the Hovertrain people really would like some extra security," says Grandad. "I feel an opportunity coming on Derek. A way to kill two birds with one stone, or in this case geese!"

"Metaphorically speaking of course," he adds, seeing my worried face.

"I don't like the sound of this," says Pru.

"Me neither," says Derek.

"Just hear me out a minute," says Grandad. "It's simple. Geese make excellent guard dogs, or guard geese. You have a herd of geese that you don't want. The Hovertrain people need extra security. The Dig people need extra security. Why don't we ask them if they want to buy your geese, to ensure site security. Simple!" he laughs clapping his hands together. "I can negotiate the deal, for a small sellers fee of course," he beams.

"If you want Vlad and his hooligan army you are welcome to them," says Pru.

"Well, it's worth a try I suppose," says Derek stroking his chin thoughtfully. "Can't be any harm in it can there?"

"That's settled then," says Grandad. "I will head down there straight away and sound them out."

"Can I come Grandad," I say with a mouthful of dippy egg and toasted soldier.

"Of course you can, but only if it is OK with your Aunty Pru."

"Yes, that is fine," smiles Aunty Pru, "I have to go to the shop for some groceries in any case."

Aunty Pru comes over to the table to clear my plate but stops mid action, sniffing the air in disgust.

"What is that horrible smell?" she says. "Derek did you step in something when you went out to get the paper earlier?"

"Not guilty," says Derek, "but something certainly smells ripe."

Monty emerges from under the table looking ashamed and prods at the kitchen door with his nose.

"Oh, Monty dear, have you got a poorly tummy?" says Aunty Pru opening the kitchen door. "Let's get you outside, poor thing. I hope you haven't got the squitters again."

"Doats on that dog," says Derek to Grandad when Pru has left the room. "Unfortunately, if he eats anything he's not supposed to it goes straight through him," he continues, attempting to fan the smell away with his newspaper. "Then its squitters for days afterwards."

I wrinkle my nose, trying not to breath too deeply and trying not to look guilty. But I can feel my face going red to the roots of my hair.

"Please may I get down from the table. I've finished my breakfast thank you," I say, just like Mum has taught

22

me.

"Of course you can pet," says Derek. "Why don't you pop your coat and boots on then you'll be all ready."

I slide down off my chair and pad down the passageway to the back door. I find my bright red welly boots at the end of a row of tall green welly boots. I wonder who they all belong to.

I lean against the wall and slip one Plimsol off and one welly boot on, being careful not to let my socks touch the floor. I then turn around and repeat the process with the other foot.

My little duffel coat is on a high hook with the other coats, I jump up several times before I manage to dislodge it, then it falls on my head. The buttons look like tiny barrels and are tricky to do up. But eventually I manage and am ready, just as Grandad and Derek emerge from the kitchen.

Chapter 3
Grandad Makes a Deal

"Right Missy, let's go," says Grandad. "Coming for the ride Derek?"

"Why not," says Derek. "I could do with some fresh air."

We manage to make it from the back door, to Grandad's Humber car before Vlad and his wives spot us. It is very old, like cars on black and white films. In the front, instead of having individual seats, it has one long bench seat, with a leather cover.

I wrinkle my nose; I don't like the smell of leather seats, they smell headachy. But I quickly squeeze in between Grandad and Uncle Derek and look for the seatbelts, but there aren't any.

I look at Grandad with my worried face, but Grandad is busy starting the engine and giving it revving noises. He then slowly maneuvers the car down the drive as the geese chase after us honking and flapping angrily at our escape.

I hear a scrabbling noise coming from the back seat and turn round in fright. Two of the brightest blue eyes look back at me, like chips of sky and a wet nose lurches forwards, followed by a very wet pink tongue, that licks the side of my face.

"Eeww!" I say.

"What on earth!" says Derek. "Harold did you know that there is a wolf in the back of your car?"

"Say hello to Oliver," says Grandad. "He is a Husky/Alsatian cross, so not technically a wolf."

"Hello Oliver," I say rubbing my face on my sleeve.

Oliver seems to take this as an invitation to join us on the front seat and tries to climb over; Derek fights him back.

"I'll open my window a bit," says Grandad, "that usually distracts him."

Grandad winds down his window and Oliver immediately sticks his head out, slobbering excitedly into the wind.

"Where did he come from?" asks Derek. "Does Doris know?"

"Yes, she knows," sighs Grandad. "I just shut Oliver in

the kitchen while I went to break the news, but Doris must have been in the garden and came in the back way. I was heading towards the breakfast room, when I heard a lot of shouting from the kitchen. There had been a bit of an incident with twelve plain buns and a tub of margarine. Doris was not impressed. Oliver must have been hungry poor chap."

"Oh dear," says Derek, "But where did he come from?"

"Well, it wasn't my fault," says Grandad. "I went to see Alan Bird, with a dozen eggs, on account of him being laid up poorly. When I get there, there's poor Alan stretched out on the sofa, with his wife, Deirdre standing over him, reading him the riot act. Apparently there had been an altercation involving Oliver and Brian the Bread."

"What happened Grandad?" I say excitedly.

"Well, according to Dierdre, what with Alan laid up and not able to take Oliver for his usual walks, Dierdre had left Oliver in the garden to amuse himself.

Meanwhile Brian the Bread was doing his rounds as usual, with his little motorbike and side car, delivering bread round the village, just like he always does.

Then Brian rides past the end of the garden and Oliver decides that he doesn't like the cut of his jib. Next minute Oliver comes racing down the garden at full pelt, clears the front gate in one leap and starts pursuing Brian up the road.

The poor lad sees Oliver chasing him and opens up the throttle to the maximum. But the motorbike is only a two stroke, and with the side car weighing him down, Oliver starts to gain on him.

Poor Brian, now fearing for his life, decides to take matters into his own hands and starts chucking the contents of the sidecar at Oliver, leaving a trail of 12 current buns, 3 whole meal Hovis and a flowery bloomer.

Of course Oliver thinks all his birthdays and Christmases have come at once! He stops his pursuit in order to gobble up the buns and Brian makes good his escape. By the time Dierdre gets to him he has finished all the buns and is half though the flowery bloomer. Unfortunately the 3 Hovis landed in the duck pond, so nothing was salvageable."

"Blimey!" says Derek, "I bet there was a big bill from the bakers shop for that little lot!"

"There was indeed!" says Grandad. "And to cap it off, every time someone goes past the garden on a motorbike or even a Vespa, Oliver thinks that chasing them will bring a reward of baked goods.

Naturally Dierdre is at her wits end. So what could I do? She's standing there threatening to call the dog warden and there's Alan practically in tears at the thought of losing his beloved Oliver. So I offered to look after

Oliver for a few days, just until Alan is back on his feet. Doris understood in the end, once she had calmed down a bit."

"He is a lovely dog right enough," says Derek.

"Soft as candy floss," says Grandad.

Grandad Changes down a gear as we round the bend and head down to Gullypot causeway. Water covers the road in front of us and stretches out into the fields. The willow trees stick out of the water each side marking where the edge of the road used to be.

"Grandad," I say nervously, "how do we get through?"

"Don't you worry Missy," says Grandad, crunching down the gears, "built like a battleship this car."

"Let's hope it floats like one," says Derek.

We enter the flooded road dead center and two waves of water roll out from the car on either side. I notice water welling up through a rust hole in the floor of the car and pick my feet up nervously.

The engine of the Humber coughs, but we are over half way across now and heading up out of the other side. The engine coughs again and Grandad puts his foot on the accelerator, pushing the old car forward at speed, out through the flood water.

As we power out of the last of it, the car puts up a wall of water on each side, drenching a couple of unsuspecting walkers, by the edge of the water.

Grandad carries on up the road without stopping.

"There we go," he says, "nothing to worry about."

I turn around in my seat and look out of the back window. The walkers are shouting and shaking their fists.

"Those people don't look very happy," I say.

"Ramblers," says Grandad airily. "They'll be alright, they're used to the great outdoors."

I look back at them again, they are definitely not looking alright, more like shaking with anger. But Grandad seems to have forgotten about them already as he has turned his attention to a little black box, with knobs and wires, under the dash board.

"What is that?" I say.

"This," says Grandad proudly, "is my birthday present from your Uncle Peter and Uncle Harvey."

"Oh, lovely!" I say "But what is it?"

"It's a radio-cassette player, cutting edge technology. Here I'll show you," he says twiddling one of the knobs, whilst swerving to avoid a pheasant crossing the road.

A blast of loud music suddenly erupts from behind the dash board. I clutch my hands over my ears and Oliver yelps and dives to the floor behind the front seats.

"Oops, bit loud," says Grandad twisting the knob round the other way.

"What an infernal racket," says Derek, "what sort of music is that?"

"That, is you're Heavy Metal music," says Grandad. "I said I wanted something with a bit of a beat and Peter got me this cassette."

"I'm more of a Frank Sinatra man myself," says Derek.

"Not every one's cup of tea," says Grandad. "I'll turn it off," he says, but accidently turns the knob the wrong way and the music blasts up at full volume, just as we round the corner into Bagford village center.

I clasp my hands even tighter over my ears as Oliver tries to burrow under the front seat.

"Turn it off!" shouts Derek, over the din.

"Whoops," shouts Grandad, "the knob's just come off, it does that sometimes."

"Well put it back on and turn the music down!" shouts Derek as we approach the church.

"Can't," shouts Grandad, "knobs dropped on the floor, I think it rolled under the seat."

"Oh look," I shout, "there is a wedding on at the church,

they've just come out for the photos! Doesn't the bride look pretty. Can we stop and look?"

"Keep driving!" shouts Derek, trying to slide down in his seat and pull his cap down over his face, "I hope Pru doesn't get to hear about this. For goodness sake Harold, wind your window up!"

We clatter through Bagford with the music blasting out of the car. Oliver has decided that he has had enough and starts to howl. We finally get to the end of the village, leaving a trail of startled bystanders behind us. Grandad pulls up on the verge and retrieves the lost knob from under the seat, re-attaches it to the radio cassette player and turns the music off.

"I think my ears are bleeding," says Derek.

"I don't think I like blood Uncle Derek," I say in a wobbly voice.

"Oh, no Molly, not really," says Uncle Derek, giving my hand a squeeze. "It's just an expression," he says, glaring at Grandad.

"All's well that ends well," says Grandad breezily, swinging the Humber back out on to the road.

The tarmac road soon gives way to a muddy track.

"Here we are!" says Grandad, swinging the car into a big gravel car-park.

Two huge Alsatian dogs erupt from a kennel, at the side of the carpark barking angrily.

"Grandad!" I cry, turning my face to his reassuring bulk.

Oliver leaps into the front of the car barking enthusiastically in return. His claws dig painfully into my lap and his tail hits me in the face.

I am not enjoying this trip out, I have been deafened, jumped on and nearly drowned and I want to go home. I can feel my bottom lip wobbling as I fight back the tears. I screw my eyes tight shut and try and think of my favourite things.

"Your dog's got it's backside in my face!" shouts Derek in disgust.

"Geet out of it!" growls Grandad as he hoists Oliver into the back seat by his collar.

"Don't worry Molly the dogs are chained up," says

Derek, once he can see again.

I open my eyes and sure enough the two dogs are straining and dancing at the end of two very long chains.

"Now then miss Molly," says Grandad, lets inspect the damage.

There is a big muddy paw print on the leg of my nice blue jeans. Grandad whips out a big handkerchief and rubs purposely at the mud.

"Good as new!" he says encouragingly.

"Yes Grandad," I say bravely looking at the smudgy mark on my leg.

There is a large brick building with a big sign over the door.

"What does the sign say?" I ask.

"Monorail UK. Strictly M.U.K personnel only beyond this point," he reads. "Well they didn't think that one through, did they," he adds.

A man in a white coat comes out of the large brick building and walks purposely over to our car. Grandad winds down his window.

"Can I help you?" says the man.

"We are looking for the person in charge," says

Grandad.

"Ah well," says the man importantly, "that would be me. Dr Retford Service; CEO and Chief Engineer of Monorail UK or M.U.K for short. Welcome to the home of the Train in the Sky."

"Derek Grey, Harold and Molly Green, at your um service," says Grandad, sticking his hand out of the car window. The man in the white coat grabs it and shakes it enthusiastically.

"My associate and I have come to offer you a unique and once in a life time opportunity, to enhance your security arrangements," says Grandad eyeing the two dogs on leads who are now lying lazily in the sun, yawning and scratching themselves.

"Oh, so you've heard about our trouble?" says the man scowling. He pulls a pipe from his top pocket and starts to pack it angrily with tobacco from a small pouch.

"We had heard through the village grapevine that there has been some unpleasantness with the archeologists at the Dig next door," continues Grandad.

"Unpleasantness!" growls the man waving his pipe in the air.

"Vandalism, terrorism, anarchy! We have had milk bottles smashed, fences broken and strange noises in the shrubbery after dark. They even broke into the outside lavatory, pulled all the toilet paper out and defecated on the floor!"

"Nasty," says Grandad

"Outrageous," says Uncle Derek.

"Desiccated?" I say, "Like in coconut slice?"

"Not quite," says Uncle Derek.

"Oh sorry," says the man, "I forgot that there were children present."

"In any case," continues the man, as he tries to light his pipe with a match, "we know who the perpetrators are, it's those hooligans next door at the Dig. Luddites the lot of them. They know full well that we can't start on phase two of the Monorail project until they have finished their excavations. So they are doing everything they can to hold things up."

"But how do you know it was them?" says Grandad.

"Hah ha!" says the man sucking angrily at his pipe. He pulls his pipe from his mouth, inspects it, mutters under his breath and shoves it into the top pocket of his white coat.

"As I was saying, we know it was them because there was a trail of toilet paper leading from the vandalized toilet cubicle, straight to their camp!" he exclaims triumphantly.

"Sure it's not kids playing a prank?" says Derek

"Not at that time of night!" says the man. "It's those archeologists all right," he spits. "They all live on site, so they have plenty of opportunity. They share three caravans and some sort of bivouac. Messing about all day in the dirt, looking at old bits of pot and glass, calling it science. This is science," he rants, sweeping his arm behind him in such a violent gesture he nearly loses his balance.

I notice a small smudge of smoke coming out of his top pocket.

"As for motive, they keep harping on about it being a 'site of special scientific interest,' that needs 'preserving for future generations.' They won't be happy until they have dug up every bit of old rubbish that was ever chucked into a hole."

"And another thing," says the man patting his top pocket distractedly, "OUCH!" he yells this last word and pulls the pipe quickly out of his top pocket and drops it on the floor. "Blasted thing was still lit," he says, as though this was the fault of the archeologists as well.

Grandad and Derek look at each other and pass a secret thought between them. The man stoops to the ground to pick up his pipe, which is now in two parts.

"Well er, to continue on the topic of your security," says Grandad. "My colleague and I, are in a position to offer you a special one-off deal, of our self-sustaining, eco-friendly, security system. All for the very reasonable price of £20."

"Yes, yes, please go ahead, we'll try anything," says the man, whilst attempting to fit his broken pipe back together. "The dogs are useless; just throw them a tennis ball and they get so excited they forget about guarding the place."

"In fact," says the man looking up with a glint in his eye, "can it be in place by tomorrow afternoon. We have a very important test run of the Hovertrain. Members of the press, representatives from the Government and other assorted VIPs will be in attendance."

"It will be our pleasure," says Grandad rubbing his hands together and smiling.

Another man wearing a white coat appears at the door of the building.

"Retford," he calls, "phone call for you. It's the Ministry."

"Oh well, must dash," says the man. "When you come in the morning just ask for Frank, our caretaker. He will show you where to go and sort you out with the payment." With that the man hurries back across the carpark and disappears into the brick building.

"That went well," says Grandad grinning. "Twenty pounds Derek! Talk about money for old rope!"

"But you didn't tell him about the geese!" says Derek with a shocked face.

"You don't bother a busy man like that with details

Derek," continues Grandad. "All they care about are results."

"Can we go and see the train now?" I say, feeling forgotten.

"Of course we can," says Derek. "But there's not much chance of seeing anything from here," he says, pointing to the high fences that run along the side of the carpark.

"How's this for an idea," says Grandad. "We could wonder down the drove and say hello to the dig people. I've met a couple of them in the Brown Bear, they seem like nice people. We would probably get a good view of the Monorail track from behind their camp. And you never know, they might be interested in a little extra security as well," he grins.

"Harold," says Derek smiling, "you really do take the biscuit!"

Chapter 4
A Glint of Gold

We leave Oliver in the car, and head off down the muddy drove. It's OK though because I have my red welly boots on and Grandad is holding my hand. His hand is big and warm and holds my little hand in a firm clasp, so I feel safe from getting lost or left behind.

The muddy drove has willow trees growing on either side. They are so big that in some places they meet overhead like the roof in a big church. The leaves are yellow and I can see the blue sky peeping through them. The smell of Autumn is all around. It smells like over ripe fruit and fallen leaves and earth.

The only sounds are our stamping boots, the singing birds and a tractor in a field far away. The wind stirs the trees and the leaves flutter down on us like confetti at a wedding.

I feel a surge of happiness swell in my chest, like a

balloon being blown up.

Then I hear more sounds, very faintly, from ahead; music, a tap tapping sound, laughter. This must be coming from the Dig people's camp.

We come to a gate with a sign nailed to it.

"What does the sign say?" I ask.

"'Factitius Archeological Research Trenches. F.A.R.T Personnel Only,'" Grandad reads. "Well they didn't think that one through did they!" he adds.

"It also says 'Danger Keep Out'," says Derek, pointing to the bit at the bottom.

"Oh, don't worry about that," says Grandad. "That's just to keep the general public away."

"We are the general public," says Derek.

But Grandad has already pushed open the gate and sailed through, with me still holding his hand and Derek following on reluctantly behind.

As the trees thin out on either side the noise of the music gets louder, along with the chatter and laughter and tapping. I smell wood smoke and something nice cooking. My tummy gurgles with hunger.

The trees clear and in front of us is the camp site. There are the three caravans and something that looks like a tepee from cowboy films. There is a jolly fire in the middle, with a big cooking pot hanging over it. There are logs for seats arranged in a circle around the fire.

Next to the camp there is a big field full of ditches with people working in them. A radio is propped on the side and the song playing is the dancing all night song[5]. It is one of my favourites, I like the beat. Someone in the ditch must like it too because they are singing along with the words.

"Grandad," I say. "What are the people doing in the ditches?"

"They call those trenches," says Grandad "and the

people are doing archeology. They are digging up what the Romans left here nearly 2000 years ago."

"Like what things?" I ask.

"Bits of pottery mostly," says Grandad. "Apparently these boffin types can learn a lot about the Romans from bits of broken pots."

"Oh," I say, as I watch Grandad lean over the nearest pile of earth, pick out a bit of what looks like broken pot, examine it and pop it in his pocket."

"Can I help you gents?" says a head and shoulders that have sprung up from the nearest trench. The whole body follows, as a young man with long hair tied back in a pony tail, emerges and pads across the grass towards us.

"Hello Burton," says Grandad.

"Harold, isn't it?" says the young man, greeting Grandad with a shake of his hand.

"Derek, Molly, may I introduce you to Dr Burton Coggles, who runs the Dig here."

"Nice to meet you," says the young man extending a muddy hand in my direction. I look at the muddy hand with my anxious face.

"Oh sorry," says the man, "I live with mucky hands, I just get so used to it," he smiles.

"What brings you this way then?" says the man turning to Grandad.

"Well, you did say to call in any time," says Grandad. "So we thought we would come and see how you were getting on."

"Marvelous," says the man. "It's always a pleasure when people show a genuine interest in what we are doing here."

"What exactly are you doing here?" asks Uncle Derek.

"This, gentlemen, is a site of special scientific interest, that needs preserving for future generations. We think it is the remains of a Roman settlement called Factitius.

We have found Roman coins that date to the second century AD. In the far trench we have uncovered a floor mosaic; this suggests a high-status Roman villa once stood here. But more work needs to be done and it is slow and painstaking. If only we had more time!" he sighs.

"More time?" says Derek.

"It's those thugs over at the Hovertrain place next door," says Burton angrily. "They are pressing the council for permission to extend their track right across this site. We have told the council that until we have had time to properly excavate this area, then building work should not proceed at this time, if at all.

But these Hovertrain people think the law doesn't apply

to them. They've started a campaign of intimidation and harassment against us. They are trying to scare us out, but we will not be moved!" says the Burton firmly.

"What kind of harassment?" asks Grandad.

"Food pinched, clothes dragged off the washing line and dragged through the mud. They even dug up a couple of the tent pegs so that the big tent collapsed. That is where the students sleep and it gave them one heck of a fright."

"Sure it isn't kids playing a prank?" says Derek,

"What at that time of night?" says the man. "In any case, we know it was them because we found Shona's brassiere caught in the hedge between us and them. It looked as if someone had tried to drag it through the gap!"

"Nasty," says Grandad

"Outrageous," says Uncle Derek.

"Brazil?" I say, "Like in the nuts we have at Christmas?"

"Not quite," says Uncle Derek.

"Oh sorry," says Burton. "I forgot that there were children present."

"Sounds like you could do with some security," says Grandad rubbing his hands together.

"What like those horrible, vicious, dogs they've got next door?" says the man. "No thank you, we are peace lovers here."

"I was thinking about something a bit more progressive," says Grandad smiling. "My colleague and I, are in a position, to offer you a one-off deal on our self-sustaining, eco-friendly, security system. All for the very reasonable price of £20…"

I begin to feel bored of the grownup conversation and feeling invisible. So I wonder towards the nearest trench.

A magpie is puling at something in the soil by the path, so I salute him and say "Good Morning Captain," so as not to get bad luck. But the magpie gets scared and flies away, 'ach, ach aching' crossly.

I go to look at what the magpie was so interested in and see a glint of gold shining up from the ground. I pull at it with my fingertips, giving it a wriggle backwards and forwards to free it from the soil. Then out pops a small gold ring with a tiny green stone. I look at it amazed, then get a tissue out of my pocket and give it a rub to get the earth off.

It shines at me in the sunlight, as fresh and bright as the day it was made. I slip it onto my finger; it fits perfectly. It must have been lost by a little Roman girl. I shine it on the tissue and admire the way it looks on my finger.

"Molly," calls Grandad.

I look up guiltily and try to take the ring off to put it back, but it's stuck. I put my hand in my coat pocket and trot over to Grandad and Uncle Derek. Burton has already gone back to his trench.

"OK Molly?" says Uncle Derek.

"Yes thank you," I say.

"Burton says we are free to explore the site just as long as we are careful not to fall in the trenches," says Grandad. "So I thought we could explore all the way to the back of the camp, where we might get a good view of the Monorail and the Hovertrain."

"Oh that will be nice," I say, wondering how I will get the ring off my finger and put it back before I get into trouble.

"They usually test it around now. They have to get special permission from the Electricity Board before they switch it on," continues Grandad to Derek.

"Good grief," says Derek, "I hope it's all worth it!"

I twist the ring round my finger in my pocket and think what the Hovertrain might look like, to take my mind of things.

I follow Grandad along the narrow path between the trenches. Uncle Derek follows on behind. I carefully peer down, and the students smile up at me. They all have little scraper tools and brushes to carefully work away at the soil in the bottom of the trench. I wonder why they don't just use a big shovel, like Dad uses to dig with in the garden. I think about mentioning this to the students, but I decide not to, as grownups can get funny about children pointing out obvious things to them.

Once we have passed the last of the trenches, we come to a mass of huge, overgrown weeds, all dead and dried out like a skeletons forest. Each stalk is hard and straight, like runner bean canes and are so tall that they even reach above Grandad's head.

The smell that comes from them is strong and musty, it makes me sneeze.

"Don't touch these ones Molly," says Grandad, "Hogweed can give you a nasty rash."

"Something's made a path through here Harold," says Derek to Grandad.

We follow the path as it winds through the Hogweed patch. On the other side there is a small stile just reaching out of an overgrown hawthorn hedge. The hedge is weighed down with bright red berries; they seem to glow against the last of the yellow leaves. With every puff of breeze a few more leaves flutter down to make a yellow carpet below.

Five swans fly low above us; they form an arrow shape in the sky and sing 'hoop, hoop, hoop' as they fly along.

Grandad helps me climb up on to the stile and the three of us lean forward to get a better view. But all I can see is a grass bank. It stretches away as far as I can see to both the left and the right.

"What is that bank for?" I say pointing.

"That's the bank for the Old Bagford Cut," says Grandad. "It's basically a man-made river. It was built four hundred years ago by a famous Dutch engineer called Edward Van Halen, to drain the land. If it wasn't for Van Halen, our village would be under nine feet of water."

"Oh," I say. "That wouldn't be very convenient!"
"Indeed not," says Derek, smiling.

"I don't see any railway lines," I say, looking around with my disappointed face.

"That's because you're not looking in the right place," says Derek. "You need to look up!"

"Wow!" I say, "It's Like on *The Thunderbirds*[6] or *Flash Gordon*[7]!"

"More like *Mission: Impossible*," [8] says Derek, smiling.

Running level with the top of the bank is a concrete beam, held up in the air by concrete pillars. It stretches to the right hand to some big sheds in the distance, and the other way just as far as the Dig camp.

A wail from a siren suddenly splits the air and a crowd of frightened crows lift up from the near by trees and flap 'cawing' in alarm, away over the campsite. I clutch Grandad's arm in fear.

"Don't worry Molly, that just means that they are preparing to run the Hovertrain down the track. It's just to let people know to get out of the way," he says. "Looks like you're going to get your wish and see the train run!"

I twist the gold ring on my finger and clutch Grandad's arm a bit tighter. In the distance, near the big sheds, I can see a big white and blue shape, like a box sitting on top of the concrete beam. It starts to move towards us, gathering speed. It gets closer and closer and quicker and quicker, with a big cloud of dust and leaves billowing out behind it. Then it is looming right towards us, huge on the rail. I can hear a metallic scraping buzz getting louder and louder with sparks like a firework shooting out from the back. It's just like Flash Gordan's ship.

It hurtles above us; there is a screech of brakes. I cry in fright and bury my face in Grandad's coat.

"It's Ok Molly," says Grandad patting my back, it's stopped now, nothing to be scared of," he says.

"Well that isn't something you see every day," says Derek, puffing out his cheeks.

"Let's just hope Mrs. Spatchcock hasn't got her Hoover out!" replies Grandad.

"Can we go now please?" I say in a small voice. I feel shaken and shivery; every inch of me is jangling. I want to get away from this strange place where spaceship trains fly though the air, showering sparks and screeching like a thousand screams. The smell of the Hogweed is overwhelming and I feel a bit sick.

"Oh dear now," says Grandad, bending down so he can

examine me. "You look a bit peaky. I think that's enough excitement for one day!"

Grandad takes my hand and leads me though the Hogweed path, back to the campsite, with Uncle Derek following on. The students and Burton have returned to their digging and take no notice of us as we pass by.

Finally, we get back to Grandad's car. The big Alsatian dogs are lying in a pool of sunshine. They snarl at us as we get into the car, but they are too lazy to bark at us again.

Grandad opens the driver's door.

"Oliver!" he exclaims. I peer under Grandad's arm and it looks like Oliver has grown a white fluffy beard, like Father Christmas.

"Woof," says Oliver wagging his tail, then he sneezes violently and the white fluffy beard flies all over the floor. He leaps excitedly into the back of the car revealing a big hole in the front seat, with white stuffing hanging out of it. A big hole that wasn't there when we left.

"Oh Oliver," says Grandad sighing.

"Sneeze!" says Oliver, trying to wipe the rest of the stuffing from his nose with his front paw. I giggle.

"What's Doris going to say?" says Grandad with a glum look.

"Reckon she'll say it's time you got a new car!" chuckles Derek.

"I think I need a strong sugared tea," says Grandad.

"What about Skippy's Cafe?" says Derek.

"Good plan," says Grandad. "Molly looks like she could do with a bite to eat and a glass of pop."

"Oh yes please," I say, although I am not keen on fizzy drinks.

"It's a deal then," says Grandad.

We all pile into the car and Grandad swings the Humber out of the car park, heading back down the track.

I am glad to be going to the cafe. Then I feel the gold ring on my finger and guilt comes over me like a hot wave and makes me feel sick.

Chapter 5
Skippy's Cafe

We park outside Skippy's Café. It used to be a railway carriage. But someone took it off its wheels, stuck it to the ground, hollowed it out and made it in to a cafe, probably someone called Skippy.

Grandad pulls a length of orange string out of his pocket and slips it though Oliver's collar.

"Not going to make that mistake again!" he says to no one in particular.

The four of us get out of the car and push through the front door of the cafe. The bell jangles loudly, but the cafe looks deserted. Then the sound of banging pans comes from behind the partition door, so we know we are not alone.

I wrinkle my nose. The place has a strong smell; a mixture of coffee, bacon and B.O. I don't think Mum would approve. But then Mum and Dad are in Yorkshire, looking at petrified waterfalls and having fun without me.

"Shop!" says Grandad slapping his hand down on the bell on the counter.

An elderly woman shuffles out of the kitchen wearing a grubby apron and a vacant expression. Her mouth looks like two folds of uncooked pastry.

"Good morning my good lady," says Grandad smiling his best smile. "We would like three of your best bacon butties, two teas and a bottle of orange pop, if we may."

The woman stares at Grandad as if he is completely mad.

A flash of uncertainty crosses Grandad's face and his smile fades.

"To eat in?" he says.

There is a very long pause as the woman stares at Grandad. Uncle Derek shuffles his feet nervously. I hold my breath.

The woman opens her pastry mouth a fraction revealing a set of toothless gums.

"Pound," she mumbles, extending a greasy hand.

"Oh yes, thank you," says Grandad rummaging

frantically in his pocket for his wallet and extracting a pound note; he places it gingerly in the woman's hand.

The woman's hand snaps shut on the pound note and shoves it in her apron pocket. She turns her back on us and shuffles back through the partition doors into the kitchen.

"Lovely," says Derek.

"Let's get a table," says Grandad.

We sit next to a window dripping with condensation. I draw a smiley face on the glass, with my finger. Oliver is very interested and makes his own drawings on the window with his nose, then licks it for good measure.

"Come on Oliver," says Grandad. "Lie down now." Grandad ties the sting, that is attached to Oliver's collar, to the table for good measure.

The door bell jangles again and two men come in. They are wearing white overalls spattered with paint. Both men have cigarettes hanging out of their mouths. The smoke smells disgusting, like when Mum plucks a chicken for Sunday lunch, then singes the stubble off it with a lighted match. I hold my nose trying not to breathe the stench in.

"A Pound is a bit steep isn't it?" says Grandad removing his hat and running his hand over his hair.

"That's inflation for you," says Derek. "Here I'll go halves with you," he says rummaging in his trouser pockets. He pulls out a shining, silver, fifty pence piece and pushes it over the plastic table cloth towards Grandad.

"Oh don't be daft," says Grandad pushing it back. "It's on me."

I watch the fifty pence piece move back across the table. It has a pattern of hands holding hands all around the edge. Derek picks it up.

"Here you go Molly, have it as your pocket money," he says sliding it across the table cloth towards me.

I pick it up, amazed at such a fortune.

"Thank you, Uncle Derek," I say, "and thank you Grandad for my food." I push the fifty pence carefully into the pocket of my jeans.

"You're welcome," says Grandad. "Mind, you haven't tasted it yet," he says giving the kitchen a sidewards glance.

"My dear departed mother used to do the best fry-ups ever," says Uncle Derek, with a faraway look in his eyes. "The secret was the pan she used; she had this cast iron frying pan, got it as a wedding present. She would cook us a fried breakfast in that pan, every Saturday morning. The secret to the flavour was that she never washed it, only wiped it clean with kitchen roll. It built up this sheen of fat and that is what gave the breakfast such an amazing taste."

"You can't beat a well proven pan," says Grandad nodding with appreciation.

"I coveted that pan," says Derek. "Asked Mother to leave it to me in her will."

"Well it takes years for a pan to build up a finish like that," says Grandad.

"In any case," continues Derek, "soon after Prudence and I were married, Mother, sadly, passed away.

After the funeral, when I took Father home, he led me solemnly into the kitchen and handed me the frying pan. He told me it had been Mother's dying wish that I should have it. I was overwhelmed. I carried that pan home like it was a new born baby. I placed it proudly on the kitchen side, then set off down to the butchers to get some bacon and sausages for a memorial fry-up.

All the way home I was thinking of that rich flavour that only Mother's pan could give, and thinking of her smiling down on me from above, as I cooked it all up."

Derek pauses and takes a deep breath.

"But it wasn't meant to be..." he says, bowing his head.

"Why, what happened?" asks Grandad.

"By the time I got back home from the butchers, Pru had been at it with a Brillo pad and some Vim. She had scrubbed that pan back to its bare metal; it looked like it had been shot-blasted."

"'Your Mother's old pan has come up quite nicely!' she said to me, brandishing it in the light from the kitchen window. The reflection from the naked metal dazzled me. Sixty years of accumulated flavour stripped off in the twinkling of an eye."

"What happened next?" says Grandad visibly shocked.

"I asked for a divorce of course," says Derek.

"Fair play," says Grandad.

"Indeed," says Derek. "I asked her if Leonardo had come home to find his wife had paint stripped the Mona Lisa? I asked her if Chippendale had brought home his finest table and chairs to find his wife had cut the legs off when he wasn't looking?"

"So what happened next?" I ask getting impatient.

"She threw the pan out of the kitchen window, told me to 'stick it up my jumper,' and stalked out of the room with her nose in the air."

"And did you get a divorce?" I ask with wide eyes.

"No, of course not," chuckles Uncle Derek. "That was thirty years ago. Me and your Aunty Pru are still married and the frying pan is still where it landed in the herb bed, under the kitchen window. The birds decided to use it as a bird bath, so it has been there ever since."

"Doris has a formidable throwing arm as well," says

Grandad. "She could have opened the bowling at Lords."

"How so?" asks Derek.

"Well," says Grandad. "When I first started keeping chickens, I was quite overwhelmed by the miracle of the egg. Every morning I would give the chickens their feed, put my hand in the nesting boxes and fish out those beautiful warm brown eggs. It was like discovering buried treasure, every time I picked one up and put it in the basket.

Every morning I would take the basket of eggs into the kitchen and say, 'Look, Doris, look what the chickens have laid, aren't they amazing, isn't it a miracle!'

In any case, one morning I go into the kitchen and Doris has the big preserving pan on the stove, molten orange and sugar bubbling away. There was another pan next to it full of boiling water for sterilizing jars and there was a big box of oranges on the table waiting to be prepared. Doris was pink from the heat and the steam, and wisps of hair were escaping from her hair-do; I should have seen the warning signs…

So I put down the basket of eggs as usual and said 'Look, Doris, look what the chickens have laid, aren't they amazing, isn't it a miracle!'

Lightening quick she spins round from the table, eyes glaring wildly, she picks up an orange and shouting 'Well look what Mama laid!' throws it at my head!"

"Extraordinary!" says Derek. "What did you do?"

"Ducked," says Grandad. "And I never mentioned the eggs again. Just left them in the scullery every morning for Doris to find."

"There go," a voice mumbles behind us, making me jump. The cafe lady's slippered feet make no noise as she shuffles across the brown stained lino that covers the floor. She wallops a tray down in front of us; the milky tea slops from the cups into the saucers. The bottle of orange pop is so orange it looks like it is glowing.

I pick up the bottle of orange. It feels warm.

"Thank you," I say in a small voice.

I can't drink warm drinks that are supposed to be cold drinks. It's like the bottle of milk we have to drink at break time every morning at school. The milkman always leaves it in the sunshine by the front of the School, so when they give it out at morning break it has got warm.

It's OK in the winter when it's cold outside. I even quite like stabbing the silver top with the plastic drinking straw. I can drink it down quickly when it's cold, without tasting it. But in the summer, you stab the top and the smell of warm milk comes out. I try and drink it but it makes me feel sick. One time I tried to leave it on the side when no one was looking. But then the teacher saw me and she got cross and told me that if I want to get crickets then that's the right way to go about it.

But I don't see what's so bad about crickets because Jiminy Cricket is a cricket in the film Pinocchio[9] and he's nice.

I told Mum what the teacher said but she said that it's not crickets, it's rickets, and it's a disease that children used to get in the olden days, that affected their bones and made their legs go wonky. She said not to worry because children these days get plenty of vitamin D, and that is what is in the milk that stops your legs getting poorly.

I tried to tell Mum that the milk makes me feel sick and that I can't drink it, but then the telephone rang and she wasn't listening to me anymore.

So now I am scared that I'll get wonky legs because I can't drink all my milk at school and I can't tell because everyone will be cross.

I twist the gold ring on my finger and it makes me feel better to feel it there. I bet Roman children didn't have to drink warm milk or warm orange pop.

The evil looking bottle of pop looks at me from the table and I look back.

Just then another tray slams down on the table in front of us, accompanied by the heavy breathing of the cafe lady. This time the tray is holding three plates with 3 bacon butties. Grandpa hands the plates out.

The bacon smells good, Oliver thinks so too because he

puts a paw on Grandad's lap and makes a small whimpering sound with his head on one side. I bite into my butty. The bread is soft and white and the bacon is crispy and salty.

Derek opens his butty and squirts ketchup onto it out of the plastic tomato shaped bottle from the table. I don't like ketchup as it makes the bread go soggy and I don't like soggy bread.

We eat in contented silence. Oliver whimpers as he sees the food disappearing from our plates. The men at the next table slurp their mugs of coffee and read their newspapers.

The door bell jangles again and another customer comes in. Just before the door closes a tabby cat nips in through the doorway. It is the same cat I saw at Aunty Pru's house, with the traffic light eyes.

The cat stiffens as it spots Oliver. Oliver spots the cat.

"Woof, woof, woof," barks Oliver excitedly as he leaps to his feet and lunges towards the cat. CRASH goes our table, as Oliver has forgotten he is tied to the table leg and pulls the whole thing over.

Luckily, I still have my butty in my hand, so that is safe. Even more luckily the evil orange pop bottle has fallen on to the floor and smashed, rapidly staining the brown lino bright orange. Somehow Grandad has landed on his back in his attempt to grab the lead and Derek appears to be wearing most of the ketchup from his butty.

The shop door blows open with a jingle and the cat loses no time in escaping though the gap. Oliver is now much more interested in finishing off Grandad's bacon that has landed on the floor just in front of him.

"I think I'd like to go home now," I say.

"Me thinks so too," says Grandad looking up at the cafe lady as she stares down at him with her arms folded and a cross expression on her face.

Chapter 6
Ride Riding Hood and the Rocking Horse

Back at Uncle Derek and Aunty Pru's house, I carefully take off my coat and red wellington boots and put on my Plimsolls. I have to hop from one foot to another to make sure my feet don't touch the ground in just my socks.

Grandad and Uncle Derek are still outside by the car chatting. My hands are still sticky from the bacon butty and I am desperate for a wee, so I head for the small toilet room next to the back door.

The toilet walls are decorated with photos of all the dogs that Aunty Pru and Uncle Derek have ever owned, always in pairs. There are spotty ones, tall ones with wavey hair, short ones with curly hair, small ones with short hair.

Most of the photos are black and white, some of the newer ones are in colour. I recognize Monty. He looks very sleek and young with no grey hair around his nose. He is sitting proudly next to another dog of the same kind, maybe a brother or a sister? I wonder what happened to the other dog, as I wash my hands and dry them on the towel.

The running water has made me realize how thirsty I am. All that salty bacon and no drink. But Mum says I must never drink water from the bathroom tap, and must only ever drink it from the kitchen tap.

I pad into the kitchen. By standing on tiptoes, I manage to reach a mug from the draining board, turn on the cold tap, and fill the mug up. The water is cold and good and I glug it down gratefully.

I don't know what to do with the mug, as I have used it now so it isn't clean. I don't want someone to use it by mistake.

"Aunty Pru?" I call out. But no one replies. I am totally alone. Alone in this big old house with its secrets and whispers in the dark. I begin to feel a bit scared.

"Aunty Pru?" I call out again in a small voice. Still there is no reply. I stand on tiptoe again and carefully put the mug in the sink. Then I stand still and strain my ears. I feel the fear prickling up my back and my palms feel sweaty.

I twist the gold ring on my finger nervously. I take a deep breath and listen extra carefully. The old house is not silent after all. There are tiny creaks and clicks and I think I can hear music from a piano.

Shakily I walk out of the kitchen and down the long hall towards the door at the end. The music gets louder as I get closer; it's coming from the living room. The big wooden door has a round brass door knob. It is cold and smooth to the touch; I grasp it in my small hand, twist it slowly and push the living room door.

I feel like I am going to faint with fear. Will the piano be playing itself? Or will there be a ghostly figure making music from a past life?

The door swings wide open and the light from the window dazzles me for a moment so I can't see.

"Hello Dear," says Aunty Pru from the piano stool, "I wondered where you had got too."

She stops playing and looks at me intently.

"Are you OK?" she says, "you look like you have seen a ghost?"

I stand speechless in the doorway, relieved beyond belief.

"Come and sit next to me," she says, "I can teach you how to play some tunes if you like."

I skip happily over to the piano and squeeze on to the stool next to Aunty Pru. She smells of bread and roses and she puts her arm around my shoulders and her warmth comforts me.

"There that's better she says."

"It's a very big piano," I say. "It feels like a ship and we are the sailors on the bridge and have to steer it."

"This is a grand piano," smiles Aunty Pru. "It belonged to my mother."

"Well it's very nice," I say, looking at my reflection in the dark polished wood.

"She taught me to play when I was about your age. Would you like to learn a tune?"

"What music were you playing when I came in before?" I ask.

"Did you like that one?" She says.

"Oh yes," I reply, "it made me feel happy and sad all at the same time."

"That's good," says Aunty Pru. "That shows you have a good ear and an appreciation for music. Here," she says handing me the music, "what does the title say?"

My heart sinks. I stare at the bold letters at the top of the page and put my finger on them to try and stop them moving around. I take a deep breath and sound out the words.

"To – A – Wild -R – O – S-E ?" I say uncertainly looking

up at her.

"That's right," she says, "*To a wild Rose*.[10] I'm glad you like it because it's one of my favourites."

"Can you teach me how to play it?" I say.

"Yes, of course," says Aunty Pru, "I can show you how to play the right hand, which are the high notes that follow the tune. Then I will play the left hand, which are the low notes that accompany it. We can make a duet out of it."

After fifteen minutes or so I am getting quite good at it, although I still get the notes wrong and then I giggle.

"You really have got a good ear!" says Aunty Pru "We will make a concert pianist of you yet. It's thirsty work though, all this practicing. Time for a cup of tea I think. Would you like tea or some lemon squash?"

"Lemon squash please," I say happily.

"OK then," says Pru. "I'll go and put the kettle on and you keep practicing."

I pick out the notes again, swinging my legs happily under the piano stool. Then I try and pick out the notes of some of the songs that me and Dad sing together.

It is nice in the large sunlit living room, with the sound of the piano and the smell of wax polish and yesterday's wood smoke. I can't imagine why I had felt so scared earlier.

On top of the piano is a collection of photos in silver frames. I realize that I am looking straight at a picture of my mum, when she was young. She is laughing with another girl, about the same age as her and a little boy. The little boy looks familiar, although he must have moved because his face is a bit blurred. He looks about the same age as me, but he is wearing old fashioned clothes, shorts and a knitted tank top. The photo is black and white, so I know it must be old.

I look closer and realize that the boy is stroking a tabby cat and it looks like one eye is a different colour to the other, although it is hard to tell when it is not a colour photo.

Aunty Pru comes back into the room carrying the drinks and some biscuits on a tray.

"Is that a photo of my mum?" I say pointing to the picture on the piano.

"That's right," says Aunty Pru putting the tray down on the table, "your mum used to come and spend a week or two with us every summer, when she was a girl. Her and my daughter Sally were like two peas in a pod in those days."

"Who is the little boy?" I ask.

"That's my son, Luke," says Pru, picking up the photo and touching the face of the boy tenderly, "but everyone called him Pilot because he was mad about aeroplanes and that is what he wanted to be when he grew up." She puts the picture back on the piano.

"He looks like you," I say.

"Yes, he does," says Aunty Pru smiling.

"I think I've seen that cat!" I say "The one in the photo that Luke is stroking."

"Well, he would be an extremely old cat if you had," Aunty Pru chuckles. "One for the record books I think!"

"Oh?" I say, puzzled.

"That was Blue, says Aunty Pru. He was one of our farm cats, a right terror, semi-wild, but Luke tamed him and in the end he followed him everywhere."

"I don't understand," I say "I'm sure I have seen Blue, he has one blue eye and one yellow eye."

"Blue had many children," says Aunty Pru, "all running wild around the farm and the villages. I think you must have seen one of Blue's great, great, great grandchildren. I occasionally catch a glimpse of them, but they never let me get close."

"Oh, I see," I say.

"Well let's have our drinks; you must be thirsty!" she says. "Derek just told me what happened at Skippy's Cafe. Honestly! Those two men shouldn't be allowed out alone!"

I giggle.

"I'd have loved to have been a fly on the wall when that dog of your Grandad's pulled the table over," she chuckles. "Although lord only knows how I am going to get the ketchup stains out of Derek's shirt!" she says as she pours her tea into a cup and hands me a glass of lemon squash.

We sit and enjoy our drinks and eat a chocolate digestive biscuit each.

"What was Mum like when she was a young girl?" I ask. I can't imagine Mum being little like me.

The sun dips down behind the trees and the room is cast into shadow. I shiver a bit.

"I tell you what," says Pru, "let's light the fire, then we can settle down on the sofa and I can tell you all about it."

Aunty Pru has already laid the fire in the grate ready to be lit. She does the same as Granny Green, scrunching up old newspaper into balls and putting small sticks called kindling in a pointy pile on top.

She strikes an extra-long match and I smell the spark as it lights. Carefully she puts the flame to the newspaper and holds it there until it catches. In a few minutes the kindling is crackling and snapping so Pru puts some bigger bits of wood on and a log.

"There, that's better," she says coming to sit with me on

the sofa. "Later, when we have got some good red embers we can toast some bread over the fire with the toasting fork."

"Oh yes please," I say, "I'd like that very much."

As we settle down on the sofa Monty appears at the door. His nails clack on the wooden floor, then he flops down on the hearth rug in front of the fire, with a contented sigh.

"Your mum started coming to stay with us for holidays when she was about your age," says Aunty Pru. "Sally and her hit it off from the start; we used to call them the terrible twins because they just couldn't keep out of mischief."

"Really?" I say, with my eyes wide, "My mum getting into mischief? But she's so serious."

"We were all young once," Aunty Pru chuckles. "Those two girls had very over active imaginations!"

"What was the naughtiest thing they did?" I ask.

"They didn't mean to be naughty," says Aunty Pru, "but they did used to egg each other on. One time they found the key to the door of the attic. The key had been lost for years. But they had got it into their heads that if they tried every old key that they could find around the house, then one of them was bound to fit. Eventually they must have found one that did.

Well up the attic stairs they went. It must have seemed

like an Aladdin's cave to them. It was stuffed with generations of my family's old toys and broken furniture and probably a kitchen sink or two.

There was an old rocking horse up there that I used to play with as a child and it wasn't new then. Goodness knows how old it was. But it still worked and the girls were thrilled.

They made up a game based on Red Riding Hood. As far as I could gather, one of them would be Red Riding Hood and ride on the rocking horse, pretending to go to Grandma's house. The other one would be the Wolf and try and stop Red Riding Hood getting to Grandma's house.

To make the game even more real they decided they should have costumes. For Red Riding Hood, they found an old red shawl in one of the trunks and paired it with a whicker shopping basket. But they couldn't find anything in the attic that was suitable for the Wolf.

Then Sally remembered my beautiful fox fur stole.

"What is a fox fur stole?" I ask.

"Well, it's like a scarf made out of the fur of a fox with its head and legs and tail preserved and intact."

I pull a frowning face because that doesn't sound very nice at all.

"Different times," says Aunty Pru as an explanation. "My father brought it for me as an 18th birthday present and I wore it to all the parties. It was very chic in the 1930s and I felt so proud and grown up. It was lined with grey silk and the foxes eyes were made of coloured glass and the fur was so soft and warm."

Aunty Pru sighs in a sad sort of way.

"But fashion and attitudes change and I hadn't actually worn it for a very long time. But as my father had given it to me and it had such happy memories associated with it, I kept it safely in the back of my wardrobe.

Sally remembered me showing it to her one time and she thought it would be perfect for the Wolf costume.

I was upstairs in my bedroom doing a bit of tidying when all of a sudden I heard an almighty crash from above. For a wild moment I thought a chimney pot must of blown over and come through the roof. Then I heard crying and running footsteps and I knew they must be in the attic.

I rushed to the stairs where I was nearly bowled over by your mum. She was shouting wildly that I must come quickly as Sally must be dead.

My heart skipped not one but a hundred beats as I ran up those stairs. I shoved through the attic door to find Sally sitting in the middle of the floor nursing a cut knee. She was most definitely not dead judging from the howling noise she was making. I rushed over to her and gave her a hug and checked that nothing was broken.

Your mum came stumbling in behind me with tears streaming down her face. I hugged them both and eventually the tears subsided enough for them to tell me what had happened.

It seems the 'Wolf' had got a bit carried away trying to stop 'Red Riding Hood' getting to Grandma's house. 'Red Riding Hood' had retaliated by trying to hit the 'Wolf' with the shopping basket, at which point she fell off the rocking horse.

It was then that I noticed my lovely fox fur discarded on the floor. One glass eye was gone, a foot was missing and the tail was hanging off. I could have wept, I really could."

"Mum and Sally shouldn't have taken it, it didn't belong to them," I say firmly.

"Well," says Pru giving my hand a squeeze, "it was a long time ago, and I think they learnt a lesson because they were always as good as gold after that."

I twist the gold ring on my finger and feel a surge of shame.

"What if someone found something that was lost and took it, would that be wrong?" I ask.

"I suppose it depends if the person tried to find out who it belonged to or not," says Aunty Pru giving me a sidelong glance.

"I see," I say feeling the colour rising in my cheeks. I sit on my hands so the ring is out of sight.

SPIT, CRACKLE, goes the fire so loudly it makes me jump. Monty raises his head slowly, snorts with disapproval and goes back to sleep.

"Pru, Pru, are you in the living room?" we hear Uncle Derek calling from the hall.

"Yes dear, in here," answers Aunty Pru.

"You never guess what I just read in the *Evening Standard,*" says Uncle Derek bustling into the living room waving a newspaper in front of him. "The BBC are coming to film the special test run of the Hovertrain tomorrow and Raymond Crust is going to be presenting it!"

"Raymond who?" says Aunty Pru.

"Raymond Crust the newsreader," says Uncle Derek.

"Is he the one that looks like the chap who runs the Post Office?" asks Aunty Pru.

"What Donald Spatula?" replies Uncle Derek. "No, you're thinking of Val Doonican the singer; on TV every Saturday night, usually wearing a cardigan and sits in a rocking chair[11]."

"Oh, I thought he was called Val Singleton," says Aunty Pru.

"Valerie Singleton?" says Uncle Derek with a look of disbelief on his face. "Valerie Singleton is the lady who used to present that children's program Blue Peter[12], always making things out of washing up bottles apparently."

"How very odd," says Aunty Pru, "but how can she look like Donald Spatula from the post office, I thought he had a beard! Honestly Derek, I really do wonder about you sometimes," she says, giving him a hard stare.

Uncle Derek sighs heavily and sinks down into an arm chair.

"In any case," he says, "the BBC will be down at Bagford tomorrow filming the Hovertrain."

"Please can we go and watch the TV people?" I ask excitedly.

"Why not," says Derek, "It so happens that your Grandad and I have a little business to transact down that way."

"Are they going to take the geese?" asks Aunty Pru.

"They certainly are," says Derek smiling.

"Oh well done Derek!" smiles Aunty Pru. "I hope they know what they are letting themselves in for," she says rising from the sofa. "Now Molly what about that toast?"

Chapter 7
Luke

I snuggle down in bed with Doggy safely in my arms. The toast was good (crisp, smokey and covered in butter). I am excited for seeing the TV people tomorrow.

Aunty Pru has promised to come and tuck me into bed when it is time for lights off, so that I can look at my Tintin book for a while first. This one is called *Tintin in Tibet*[13] and it's one of my favourites.

Tintin and Snowy and Captain Haddock have gone to Tibet to rescue their friend and they have lots of adventures on the way.

So far I have collected six Tintin books altogether and I hope to get another one for my next birthday. I can't really read all the words, but I can follow the story from the pictures, which are ace. When I grow up I want to travel and have adventures like Tintin.

I hear footsteps on the stairs and along the corridor and Aunty Pru puts her head around the door.

"Only me," she says, "how's Tintin getting along, has he fallen down many crevasses?"

"Only one," I reply.

"I am pleased to hear it," she smiles, "are you ready for lights out?"

"I think so, I say in a small voice clutching doggy to me," then I remember the little boy's room along the landing.

"Tomorrow," I say, "would it be OK to play in the little boy's room along the corridor, the one with all the toys, do you think he would mind?" I ask.

"Oh," says Aunty Pru, biting her lip.

"I didn't touch anything," I say hurriedly "It's just that the door was open and I could see the teddy bear's eyes and I just wanted to have a little look. I'm sorry if I have done something wrong."

Pru sighs and takes my hand and looks at me with sad eyes.

"You haven't done anything wrong love," Derek and I are enjoying having you here. It's lovely to have a child in the house again. This house was made for children.

But since Sally emigrated to Australia, it is very unlikely that we will hear the pitter patter of tiny feet any time soon."

She sighs heavily and looks at me as if she is trying to decide something.

"The room with all the toys belonged to Luke," says Aunty Pru, looking down and picking at a thread on the quilt.

"The little boy in the photo on the piano with Mum and Sally and Blue the cat," I say.

"That's right," she smiles. "The photo was taken just before," she hesitates, "Well the thing is he died." She says looking at me sadly.

"Oh," I say with wide eyes, "What happened to make him die?"

"Whooping cough," she says shaking her head. "There was no vaccine for it in those days. Sally caught it from school and was quite ill but quickly recovered. Luke must have caught it from Sally, he got ill and he never recovered."

"I'm sorry, Aunty Pru," I say feeling my lip quiver and my eyes sting with the tears that I know are just behind them.

"It was all a long time ago," says Aunty Pru, "but I still miss him every day and wonder what sort of man he would have grown into."

I give a loud sniff as I try and stem the weepy feelings. Pru gives me a hug.

"Please don't be sad," she says, "Just as long as we remember people, they are never really gone."

I nod my head, but can't stop the tears stealing down my face.

"I think that Luke would have liked it if you played with his toys. I just couldn't bear to clear his room after it happened, so I think it would be lovely if you got some use out of his things."

"Does that mean that I can play with the toys tomorrow?" I ask rubbing my sleeve across my face.

"Yes of course," says Pru.

Aunty Pru tucks me in and turns the light off. She leaves the door open a crack and heads off back down stairs.

My eyelids feel heavy so I snuggle down into the bed. The images of the day flit through my mind, the geese, the cat, Oliver and the Hovertrain. Then I think about Luke, the little boy in the photo and I imagine I can hear a little boy laughing, somewhere away down the landing. Or is it real? But I am too tired to care and I drift off to sleep.

Chapter 8
Some Very Angry Geese

I wake with a jolt. There is a terrible noise coming from the garden. I grab Doggy and slide out of bed onto the floor. I pad across to the curtains and pull them aside to let the daylight stream in.

There is a bright blue sky, but everything in the garden is covered with frost. It looks like someone has gone mad with an icing bag and made the world into a wedding cake. Every leaf, twig and blade of grass is covered with white.

"Jack Frost has been," I say to Doggy.

There is a spider's web on the outside corner of my window. Frozen drops of water hang from silken threads like a diamond necklace.

The terrible noise continues from the spinney at the bottom of the garden. A combination of honking, hissing barking and shouting.

Grandad's Humber car is parked casually on the driveway with the front wheels on the grass.

The sounds of battle between man and geese continue. Monty breaks from the cover of the trees and comes lolloping across the paddock. Eyes wide and ears back, he makes a beeline for the open back door.

Grandad and Uncle Derek stagger from the trees carrying a huge, square, wicker basket, with a lid. They huff and puff their way across the lawn, their breath rising in the cold air like the steam from a train.

"Put it down a minute Harold," calls Uncle Derek, "I need to catch my breath!"

Angry noises come from inside the basket. I see the tip of an orange beak stab through the gap between the basket and the lid. It bites in a frenzy at the thick leather strap that is holding the lid down.

"We'll have to put one basket in the boot and the other on the roof rack," Grandad calls to Derek over the noise.

I rush from the window and hurry to put on my clothes and brush my hair. I'm scared they will leave without me and then I'll miss out on the TV people.

My clothes seem intent on slowing me down and my cardigan buttons itself up wrong. My hair is also against me and seems to have made even more knots in the night. I find my bobble hair band and tug my hair into a pony tail.

My Plimsolls put up a fight, but eventually I get them on and race down to the kitchen.

Grandad and Derek are already sitting at the table looking red in the race and a bit sweaty. Grandad pulls his trilby hat from his head and wipes his forehead with a handkerchief.

"Well hello Miss Molly," he says when he sees me, "are you ready to see the people from the BBC?"

"Oh yes," I say excitedly.

"Maybe you'll get on the television," says Derek.

"Television indeed," says Aunty Pru landing the teapot on the table. "Highly overrated if you ask me."

"You are coming with us aren't you Pru?" asks Derek.

"Wouldn't miss it for the world," smiles Pru. "In any case someone needs to make sure you too are properly supervised after yesterday's fiasco," she says.

"What's a fiasco?" I say.

"Sort of Spanish dance isn't it?" says Derek winking at Grandad.

"No, Derek you're quite wrong," says Aunty Pru, plopping a boiled egg and toasted soldiers in front of me, "the Spanish dance is a Fandango."

"Fandango or Flamenco?" says Grandad, "That is the question."

"I know what a Flamenco is," I say proudly, plunging my toasted soldier into my boiled egg. "It's a big pink bird with long legs!"

Grandad makes a choking noise and Derek looks like his tea has gone down the wrong way.

"That's right Molly," says Aunty Pru giving them both a hard stare. "What do these two idiots know."

After breakfast I go upstairs with Aunty Pru, so that I

can clean my teeth. She helps me with my hair, carefully brushing out all the knots and putting the bobble band back on into a tidy pony tail.

"There that's better," she smiles at me in the bathroom mirror, "Ready to go?"

"Oh yes!" I say excitedly

Chapter 9
A Mystery Solved

When we get out to Grandad's Humber car, Grandad and Derek are already waiting for us.

There is one basket tied on the roof of the car, and the other sticking out of the boot.

The geese have calmed down to an angry muttering; beady eyes pressed to any available gap in the basket walls, glaring out at their captors.

Derek gets into the front seat of the car with Oliver and Grandad. Me and Aunty Pru get into the back. Oliver is very pleased to see us. What's more he has only managed to chew his way through half of one of the floor mats.

The Humber coughs into life and we swing down the

drive and out of the front gates. Grandad explains to Aunty Pru that he always puts the clutch in down the hill as it saves on petrol. Aunty Pru looks pale and grabs on to the side of the seat.

Oliver tries to sit upright between grandad and Derek. But his feet scrabble for grip on the seat as Grandad whizzes around a sharp bend.

I giggle as it does look funny.

"Dear god," whispers Aunty Pru. I look round at her to find she has her eyes closed.

Eventually we swing on to the Hovertrain car park, creating a shower of gravel.

"Here we are," booms Grandad.

I look excitedly out of the window. Already in the carpark are several white vans with "BBC" printed on them. People with clip boards and cables and important looking equipment are all standing around looking busy.

The two Alsatian dogs come rattling towards the car on their chains. Oliver takes fright and plunges over the front seat landing half on aunty Pru and half on me.

"For goodness sake!" she says through a mouth full of tail and pushes Oliver off her lap. She flings open the car door and marches straight towards the Alsatian dogs.

"ENOUGH" shouts Pru glaring at them. The two dogs shudder down to the ground under her gaze and crawl forward towards her on their tummies.

Aunty Pru fishes in her coat pocket and throws them a dog biscuit each. "Good boys," she says, "now in your beds." With that the two dogs go trotting back to their kennel.

Uncle Derek and Grandad stare at Aunty Pru in amazement.

"What are we all waiting for, Christmas?" says Aunty Pru. Those baskets won't unload themselves."

I look up to the top of the car, where the basket fastened to the roof is beginning to sway from side to side with the battering from angry wings coming from inside.

"Molly and I will go on ahead and take a look at the Dig," she says.

With that she takes my hand and sails out of the carpark with me in tow.

"Those two men," she mutters under her breath, "drive me to vexation."

"Aunty Pru," I gasp, "please can we slow down a bit, I'm getting a stich."

"I'm sorry Molly," she says turning to me with a concerned look, "sometimes I forget myself. I always find a brisk walk helps when I am feeling out of sorts. Now then, where is this famous archeological dig?"

"Down there through that gate with 'Danger Keep Out' written on it," I say, "But Grandad said it was OK for us to go through."

"I bet he did," says Aunty Pru pushing the gate open. We walk down the muddy track. It is so cold that the puddles are frozen, but they break with a satisfying crack when I step on them.

"Isn't it beautiful," says Aunty Pru, waving in the direction of the fields to the side of the track. The sun is up higher now and the frosted trees glitter in the light.

"Smell that air," she says inhaling deeply. "As crisp and clear as a Swiss Alp."

We hear voices faintly in the clear air. As we get closer to the Dig, the voices get louder and they don't sound happy. The camp comes into view as we round the corner. Everything is in a big mess.

One of the girls is crying and the others are crowding around Burton, angrily waving various pieces of muddied clothing at him.

"What on earth is going on?" says Aunty Pru as we arrive on the scene.

"That man in the middle is Burton, he is the one in charge. The rest are his students, they do the digging," I say feeling full of importance.

"Right," says Aunty Pru briskly advancing on the crowd.

"Anything we can do to help?" asks Aunty Pru in a commanding voice.

"Hello," says Burton in a strained voice, taking his chance to escape from the angry students. "And you are?" he says extending a grubby hand in Aunty Pru's direction.

"Prudence Grey," she says shaking his hand firmly. "I'm Derek's wife, I believe we are expected."

Burton looks confused.

"I understand that my husband Derek Grey and his associate Harold Green are handling your security arrangements," continues Aunty Pru.

"Oh, thank goodness," says Burton, he looks like he is about to cry. "Once more our perimeter has been breached and our humble camp desecrated by those animals from next door!" he cries, waving his hands around.

"We awoke this morning to total carnage. The clean washing we left to air by the fire, has all been pulled down in the night and trampled into the mud. Holes have been dug in the open trenches and as for the mosaic," he sputters, "something unspeakable has happened!"

"Show me," says Aunty Pru briskly. Burton leads the way to a large open hole at the far end of the site.

"There," he says pointing a quivering finger into the hole. "This is a second century floor mosaic depicting Cupid riding a dolphin and as you can see someone … someone has defecated on Cupid's head!" he wails.

"Well really!" says Aunty Pru.

Burton looks up with wild eyes "It's those vile creatures from the Hovertrain. They are intent on driving us away so that they can extend their beastly Monorail. We should have finished the digging season two months ago, but we dare not leave. Now the ground is freezing up and the University is threatening to cut our funding if we don't find something significant soon. How much more significant can you get than this beautiful mosaic? What more do they want? A perfectly preserved amphitheater? A triumphal arch? Or maybe an obelisk or two!"

I can tell that Burton is working himself up into what Aunty Maggy would call a blue funk. Meanwhile Aunty Pru has stepped down into the hole and is inspecting Cupid's head, with the help of a pointy stick.

"Badgers," she says looking up at Burton.

"Badgers what?" says Burton.

"Badgers causing all this chaos; badger poo on Cupid's head, badger tracks in the mud by the washing, and a badger set over there under the hedge," states Aunty Pru.

Burton looks confused.

"So it's not the Hovertrain people then?" he asks.

"Certainly not," says Aunty Pru, "Not the Hovertrain people or aliens from the moon or a government conspiracy, just badgers foraging for food."

"Oh," says Burton looking deflated.

"I expect they have had a set here for years," says Aunty Pru. "It looks like it is you that has invaded their territory."

"Where do you want these geese then?" calls Grandad, as he advances on the camp with uncle Derek. Between them, and with some effort, they are carrying a large and angry wicker basket.

"Geese?" says Burton, looking like a man who is about to lose his mind.

"That's right, they are the extra security that you ordered," says Grandad undoing the buckles on the leather straps. "We promised you a self-sustaining, eco-friendly, security system. Well here they are!" he says opening the lid with a flourish.

An angry whir of wings and beaks explode out of the basket and rearrange themselves into four of Vlad's wives. In a rage of honking and hissing they race into the camp.

The students scream. Burton screams and accidently steps backwards into the hole landing on top of Cupid, his dolphin and the pile of badger poo. I hear a small sob from below.

The geese hurtle along the track through the hogweed, squeeze through a gap in the hedge and disappear over the river bank.

"Must have been able to smell the water," says Derek.

"Hope you got the money up front," says Aunty Pru.

"Well at least the Hovertrain people seemed happy with Vlad and the other three geese," says Grandad. "Of course I only spoke to the caretaker, everyone else was busy with the BBC."

"Probably the badgers making a mess over there as well," says Aunty Pru.

"What badgers?" asks Uncle Derek and Grandad. Aunty Pru tells them of her recent discovery.

"We did agree sale, no return, for the geese?" Derek asks Grandad.

"We certainly did," says Grandad.

"There we go then, all's well that ends well," says Derek.

"If only I could believe that were true," says Aunty Pru raising an eyebrow.

"In any case, if Molly wants to see the BBC then we had

better get into position on the bank," says Grandad hurriedly.

The three grown-ups start off towards the hogweed path. But I hesitate remembering the gold ring on my finger. I twist it round, looking at the lovely green stone. I hold my hand up to let the sun sparkle against it one last time.

I know it is time to give the ring back, but my mouth feels dry and my tummy feels churney. What if I get told off for taking it in the first place?

I feel something soft and warm rub against the back of my legs. I look down and Blue looks back, with his traffic light eyes staring up at me.

Very slowly I reach my hand down and stroke the top of his head. He arches his back and purrs richly, leaning into my hand.

"Thank you Blue," I say.

He blinks his blue/yellow eyes at me then cocks his head on one side as if listening to a silent call. Then he quickly trots off across the Dig site and disappears in the trees on the other side.

The sobbing in the mosaic hole has stopped and the students have retreated to the camp to retrieve their trampled washing.

"Mr. Burton?" I call softly into the hole, are you still there?"

"Yes," says a shaky voice, I'm here."

I take a deep breath, my heart thumping in my chest.

"When I was here with Grandad and Uncle Derek yesterday, I found something," I say.

"I didn't mean to take it. I put it on my finger to see what it would look like and then it wouldn't come off and then it was time to go and then it was too late to say." I give the ring a firm twist and it comes off my finger and sits there shining in my small hand.

Burton stands up in the hole and comes over to me.

"Found what exactly," he asks curiously.

"This," I say opening my hand and offering him the gold ring. "I think it's very magic." I say handing it over to Burton.

"Very magic indeed! he says excitedly examining the ring "Where abouts exactly did you find it?"

"Over there by the path," I say, "Although it wasn't really me that found it, it was a magpie."

But Burton is no longer listening.

"I knew it!" he exclaims. "This is the evidence we have been looking for. This proves it was a high status site. We're saved!" He stumbles out of the hole and runs towards the students. "We're saved! We're saved!" he yells as he runs towards them.

I shrug my shoulders. I can hear Aunty Pru calling me so I skip towards the hogweed path feeling that a great weight has been lifted from my shoulders.

Chapter 10
The Man from the BBC

"There she is," says Grandad as I reach the stile in the hedge. "Come and climb on the top rung, then you will get a good view."

I stand on the top rung with one hand on Grandad's shoulder and one on Derek's shoulder, so that I am as tall as they are.

"Is this what it feels like to be grown up?" I say "Don't you feel giddy all the time?"

"I guess you sort of grow into," says Grandad, "slowly, so that your brain has time to adjust."

"Look down there," says Pru. "The BBC people are coming down the bank!"

"And there's Raymond Crust!" says Derek. "He looks a lot shorter in real life."

"He looks nothing like Donald Spatula from the Post Office," says Aunty Pru.

Uncle Derek opens his mouth, thinks better of it and closes it again.

Raymond Crust is striding along the bank towards us. He is wearing a grey mackintosh with a matching buckle belt. He has black framed glasses and a serious expression.

He stops a little way away from us and starts pointing with a rolled-up umbrella. He is using it to boss around the other three people with him.

"That one at the back is the cameraman," says uncle Derek. The man has a big filming camera over his shoulder, attached to a tripod. It is nearly as tall as he is and looks very heavy. The man is pink in the face and his hair has stuck to his head with sweat and he looks cross.

"That's what they call a soundman," says Uncle Derek pointing to the other man. The soundman also looks cross. He is holding a long pole with what looks like a stuffed sock on the end, covered in fur. He has a headset on and is twiddling the knobs on a box on a strap around his neck.

The last person is a lady with a clipboard. She looks very fed-up and very cold as she is only wearing a small coat, a skirt, with thin tights and shoes. The shoes are spattered with mud and grass. She looks like she could do with a cup of tea.

"Come along Robert," says Raymond to the cameraman. "Why must you always dawdle along?"

"No, Jeffrey not there, here," Raymond points to the ground with his umbrella. "I will have my back to the Monorail and do my piece to camera as the Hovertrain advances up the rail behind me."

"Casandra, where are my lines. Really you must learn to keep up!" He says snatching the clipboard from the lady.

Raymond continues to boss them around until he has his back to the Monorail track, with the other three in position in front of him. He then begins to say the same lines to the camera over and over again.

The wail of the siren splits the air. I feel a shiver of excitement and promise myself that this time I won't be scared when the train speeds past. We all turn our heads in the direction of the distant hanger and see the blue and white train slowly emerge. The train is followed by a crowd of white coated scientists looking very important with clipboards and walkie-talkies.

The siren wails again and we hear a familiar series of angry honks coming from the hedge, just beyond where Raymond and the camera crew are standing. The honks get louder until Vlad bursts from the undergrowth, wings out like an angry angel, closely followed by three of his wives.

Vlad is obviously having a bad day, what with being bundled into a basket at dawn, separated from half his wives, then abandoned in a strange place. Now someone is disturbing his peace with an ear-splitting siren. Vlad looks like he has had enough and he is looking for someone to blame.

His beady eyes lock on to Raymond Crust and his camera crew. With a honk and a flap Vlad leads the charge. Just in front of us Vlad's lost wives re-appear over the river bank. They are overjoyed to see Vlad once more and rush forward to meet him. Raymond Crust and the camera crew stand glued to the spot in terror, trapped in between the two armies of geese, with nowhere to go.

"Looks like an advance on both fronts," observes

Grandad casually.

"Derek, can't you do something!" says Aunty Pru in horror.

"Too late," says Derek

Vlad is now within spitting distance of Raymond Crust, neck extended, beak open and hissing like a python.

"Get away from me!" wails Raymond. "I'm from the BBC!"

He drops the clipboard and umbrella and tries to kick out at Vlad, but Vlad is too quick and latches his beak onto Raymond's left calf, just below the knee.

"Owwwww! HELP!" yells Raymond. The cameraman and the soundman take one look at the advancing wives, abandon their equipment and run as fast as their legs will carry them up the bank and under the concrete Monorail and away down the other side.

"Cowards!" shouts Raymond, "Traitors! Owwww!"

Vlad is flapping his wings in order to batter poor Raymond as well as bite him at the same time.

"Shouldn't we try and help him Grandad," I say anxiously.

"Nooo," says Grandad. "These BBC correspondents are specially trained for this sort of thing. They are used to reporting from war zones and natural disasters and the like."

"Raymond looks like he is crying," I say.

"Casandra help me please," wails Raymond.

"RIGHT!" says the lady. "I've had enough of this. I'm cold, I'm tired, my best shoes are ruined and I want to go home!" With that she strides over to Raymond. In one quick maneuver she grabs Vlad around the neck, just below the head, pulls him off Raymond's leg and hurls him several yards across the grass. Vlad lands with a bump and a very surprised expression.

We all clap our hands.

"Well done that girl!" shouts Aunty Pru.

"Perfect technique!" shouts Grandad.

"First round knock-out!" shouts Derek.

The lady turns to us and smiles.

"Girl Guides Farmer Badge; I knew those skills would come in handy one day!" she says.

"My leg," Raymond whimpers from where he has collapsed on the ground. "I think it's broken."

"Nonsense," says Cassandra, pulling him up by the arm, "nothing that a plaster and a couple of Aspirin won't fix."

"Come along now we are going home. Then you can buy me a steak dinner, with starter and pudding and a new pair of shoes."

"Yes of course," mumbles Raymond gathering up his umbrella and clipboard from the mud.

Meanwhile Vlad retreats to the embrace of all his wives, with much wing waving and neck shaking and general outraged muttering.

In the distance the white and blue train is gathering speed. We can see the cloud of dust and the sparks showering from the back. We hear the metallic buzz as the train looms closer.

This latest intrusion is all too much for Vlad. As the train draws near he pushes out his chest and stretches himself to his full height, flapping his wings, honking loudly, as if about to charge.

Raymond turns in terror.

"Noooo!" he wails hurling his umbrella in the direction of Vlad.

But Raymond isn't very good at throwing. We all watch open mouthed as the umbrella sores through the air and clatters into the electric bits at the back of the passing Hovertrain.

There is an almighty bang and flash of light. The train slows rapidly and grinds to a halt. The air is full of white smoke and the smell of burning.

Vlad and his wives run swiftly away over the bank, while Raymond Crust stands gulping like a gold fish.

"Looks like a short circuit," says Grandad, as he helps me down from the stile. "Time we were on our way," he says grabbing my hand and leading me down the hogweed path.

"Come along Derek," says Aunty Pru. "Harold's right, it is definitely time we were going."

I look back in time to see Raymond and Cassandra hurrying after us, as a band of angry looking scientists run towards the broken train.

We emerge from the hogweed path and make our way across the Dig site. Burton and the students have lit a fire. They are all dancing around it singing the funky fighting song[14] along to the radio and doing all the actions. Burton is waving a mud-stained vest around his head.

"Bandits. Saboteurs. Luddites!"

I look behind me; Retford Service, is struggling over the stile in the hedge, closely followed by the rest of the scientists with faces like thunder. They have nearly caught up with Raymond and Cassandra, but they manage to escape by diving for cover, into the nearest trench.

"Look at them!" shrieks Retford, pointing to Burton and the students, as he busts from the hogweed path. "They've blown up the Hovertrain, now they are doing a victory dance! Well we'll soon rain on their parade! CHARGE!"

With that the white coated men come whirling into the Dig camp, just as we make it safely to the exit road on the other side.

My last sight of the camp is of Burton trying to fend off Retford with the aid of his grubby vest, while his students mount a counter attack on the scientists, with the aid of a washing line pole, a soup ladle and variously sized trowels.

"My money's on the students," says Derek, gasping heavily for breath, as we reach the road.

"Why do all our days out end up with us running away from people fighting, Grandad?" I ask feeling shaky.

"No idea," says Grandad, removing his hat and using it to fan his sweaty brow. "I must admit I have seen a lot of fights, but I have never, personally been involved in one!" he says proudly.

We finally make it back to the Humber.

Oliver is very pleased to see us. He has managed to chew the gearstick and the hand-break, so now both are covered in teeth marks and drool.

Chapter 11
A Happy Surprise

I'm feeling much better by the time we get home. My head is resting against Aunty Pru, and she has her arm around my shoulders in a comfortable way.

To my surprise, Mum's Mini-traveler car is in the drive way. I feel a surge of excitement and lean over the front seat to see. We pull up on the drive behind them and they get out of the car.

"Mum, Dad!" I call with joy, bouncing up and down on the seat. Dad opens the car door and I fly into his arms.

"Miss me?" he says smiling.

"I thought you would be away for days and days," I say. "I have been a brave girl all the time, even though Uncle Derek had a killer gander called Vlad, then Grandad sold

Vlad to the Hovertrain people and the Dig people, along with his wives. Then Vlad bit Raymond Crust from the BBC, then the Hovertrain blew up, then everyone was fighting and we had to run away."

"Just your average day out with your Grandad Green then," says Dad smiling.

I look up at Mum expecting her to have her cross face on, but she is smiling a secret smile all to herself.

"We came back early, so we could tell you the news," she says holding her hand out to me.

"Happy or sad news?" I say taking her hand.

"Very happy news," she says hugging me close. "We're going to have a baby!"

"A baby what?" I say, with thoughts of foals and lambs rushing into my head.

"A baby brother or sister for you, silly!" say's Mum

"When do we get the baby Mum?" I say excitedly?

"The baby will be coming in the Spring," she smiles, "all being well."

"Wow!" I say. "That is the best surprise ever!" I beam.

"Congratulations darling!" says Aunty Pru kissing Mum on the cheek.

Derek and Grandad have gathered around Dad doing handshaking and back slapping, like men do. Then they all swap and Pru is hugging Dad and Grandad and Derek are kissing Mum on the cheek.

In the midst of all the hugging and laughing and congratulating, I stand in my own happy bubble, taking it all in.

I go to twist the gold ring on my finger, then remember that it's not there. But I smile because it has already done its magic and I don't need it any more.

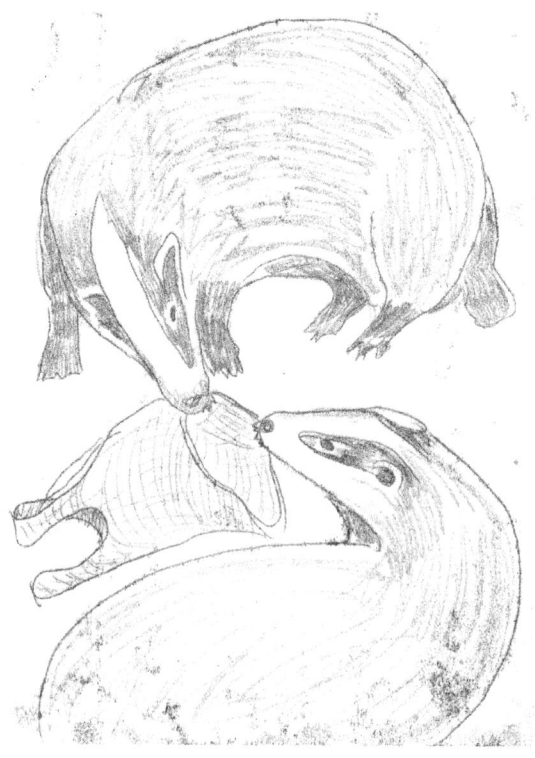

References

1. The Sound of Music. 1965 [Film] Robert Wise. dir. USA: 20th Century Fox.
2. Doctor Who. The Sea Devils. 3rd series of season 9. 1972: BBC [TV].
3. Star Trek. 1966 – 1969: Desilu Productions, Paramount Television [TV].
4. The Shipping Forecast 1924 to date: BBC [Radio]
5. Sayer, L and Poncia, V. 1976. You Make Me Feel Like Dancing. Leo Sayer [Vinyl] Chrysalis.
6. The Thunderbirds. 1965 – 1966: AP films for ATV [TV]
7. Flash Gordon's Trip to Mars. 1938 [Film Serial] Ford Beebe, Robert F. Hill, Frederick Stephani. dir. USA: Universal Pictures.
8. Mission: Impossible. 1966-1973: Desilu Productions, Paramount Television [TV].
9. Pinocchio. 1940 [Film] Supervising Directors Ben Sharpsteen Hamilton Luske. USA: Walt Disney Productions.
10. MacDowell, E. 1896.To a wild Rose. [Sheet Music for Piano] Breitkopf and Härtel.
11. The Val Doonican Music Show, 1975–1986. BBC
12. Blue Peter. 1958 – present. BBC
13. Hergé. 1962. Tintin in Tibet (Translation). UK: Methuen
14. Douglas, C. 1974. Kung Fu Fighting. Carl Douglas [Vinyl] Pye.

Acknowledgements

The Bug: thank you for the pan story.

Barty: thank you for the stories about Oliver the dog.

Richard: thank you for your advice about the ending. Vlad will live to fight another day.

May: thank you for being my proofreader.

The Hovertrain was real. Tracked Hovercraft Ltd had its headquarters at Earith in Cambridgeshire. Here they constructed a full-scale test track: a concrete monorail along the Old Bedford River. The project was begun in 1969, but the funding was cut in 1973.

About the Author

Lily Beetle exists entirely in my own imagination. She lives in a converted telephone exchange, in a dot of a village, somewhere on the River Lark. She shares her home with Pepper, her Jack Russel dog and Time and Tide, two orphaned crows that she raised from chicks.

Her next Molly book will be something about goats, but she hasn't quite decided what yet.

The first Molly book, "The Brief Fame of Attila the Hen" is available on Amazon

I hope you enjoy her stories.

Printed in Great Britain
by Amazon